# Baseball
## Coloring Book

**Coloring Pages Studio**

# Coloring Pages Studio

ISBN-13: 978-1539630562
ISBN-10: 1539630560

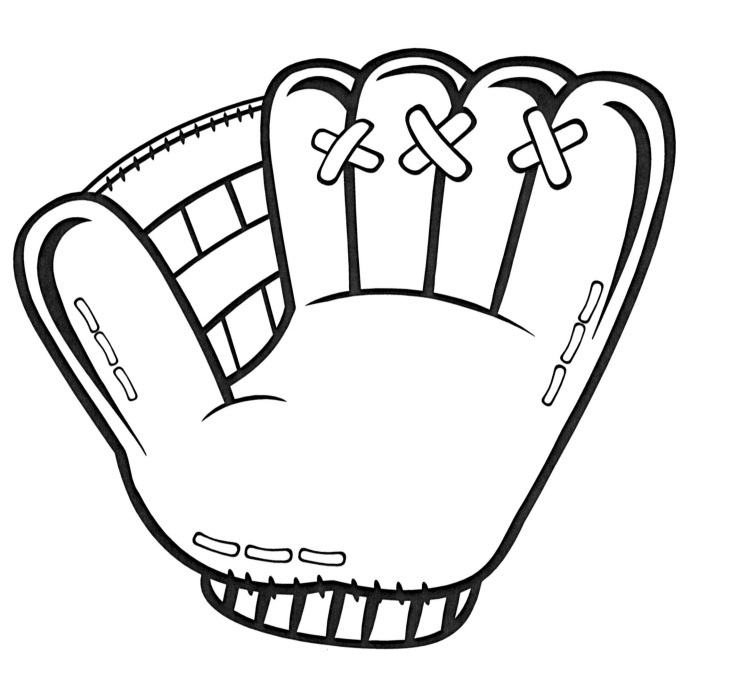

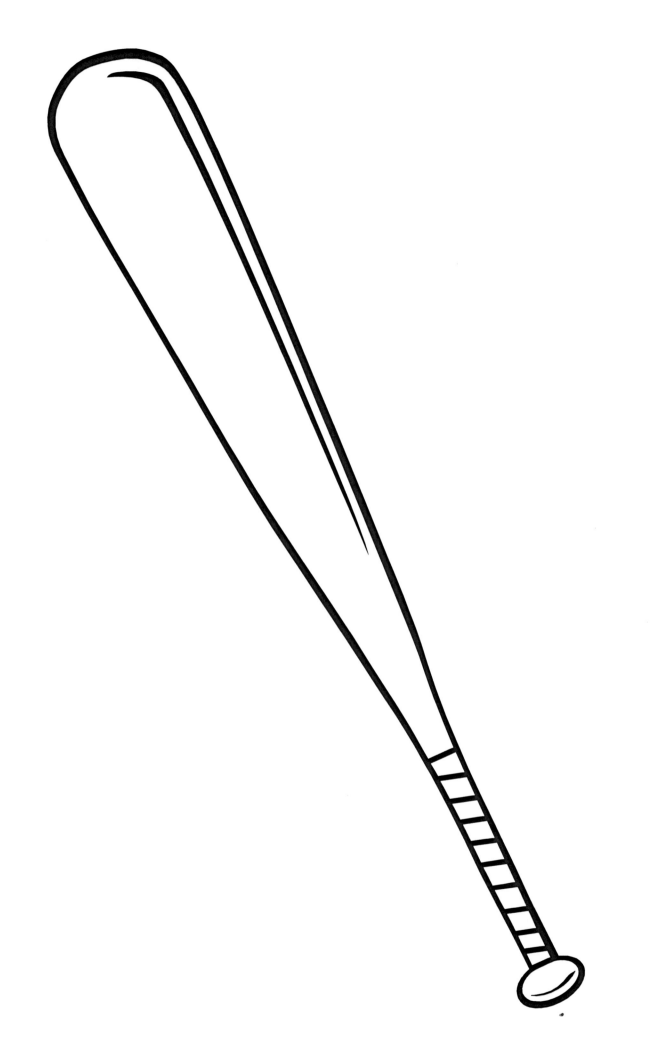

CPSIA information can be obtained
at www.ICGtesting.com
Printed in the USA
LVOW09s0925181216
517817LV00007B/326/P